MW01244179

To Haiku'm It May Concern

Living Your Best Life Even When Mecury Is In Retrograde

.

Harvey Fitz

Published by

Great Publishing Company LLC

Founders of N.U.S.P.A.

(The National Underground Spoken Word & Poetry Awards)

Alexandria, VA 22310

info@greatpublishing.com

www.greatpublishing.com

First Edition, 2021

Register of

copyrights

Library of congress catalog card number

Cover Design by Kazakura

Layout by KaNikki Jakarta and Sir Harvey

Fitz ISBN # 978-1-7333665-4-0

Printed in the United States

Publisher's Note

To Lorna, thank you for cultivating the seed.

CONTENTS

CHAPTER 1 LIVE

Harvey Fitz

TO HAIKU'M IT MAY CONCERN
Living Your Best Life Even When Mercury is in Retrograde

You've got two
choices: sit in the pain
and wallow or get up
and LIVE

1

Harvey Fitz

The truth can't set you

free until you

acknowledge

that you're a hostage

Harvey Fitz

Letting your food get
cold while watching someone
else eat is self-torture

Your rock bottom will

give you the lessons to

teach

from your mountain top

Shouts out to
fellow creatives
with 9-5's it will
be worth it

TO HAIKU'M IT MAY CONCERN
Living Your Best Life Even When Mercury is in Retrograde

The anointing hit
different when you aren't
sleeping
with your flock Bishop

[Pastor] [Deacon] [Reverend] [Elder] [Preacher]

6
Harvey Fitz

The best method of

teaching people how to

treat you is self-respect

Harvey Fitz

Life becomes a walk
in the park when you learn
how to stand in your truth

Harvey Fitz

Dear creative your
price is based on your value
versus their budget

Stop letting people
who forfeit their dreams project
their fears into you

Don't ever have a

moment of silence for

me I was loud AF

Harvey Fitz

When your name is in
rooms that your feet have never
stepped foot inside of . . .

Harvey Fitz

There is more to life
than brown liquor and crab
legs go see what's out there

You were put on this
planet to do more than
just pay bills and lose weight

TO HAIKU'M IT MAY CONCERN
Living Your Best Life Even When Mercury is in Retrograde

Don't congratulate
me if you really don't like me
I'm good love thanks

Harvey Fitz

Worry about your

sins because God's not gonna

ask you about mine

I pray y'all get blessed

with that Vanna White type

of

tenure and fortune!

Harvey Fitz

The grind is always
hiring you just have
to be willing to work

Harvey Fitz

If my handicap

bothers you then you are

the

one who's disabled

Harvey Fitz

If someone's life
makes you feel
uncomfortable then
stop watching them

Harvey Fitz

You have to learn how
to leave people right where they
had you fucked up at

Courage is fear that
finally says fuck it
my destiny awaits

Harvey Fitz

TO HAIKU'M IT MAY CONCERN
Living Your Best Life Even When Mercury is in Retrograde

Please don't let strangers
outdo you when it comes
to supporting your friends

—Hashtag you can't beat
God giving but you can
beat John & Jane Doe though!

23
Harvey Fitz

Good morning sunshine
whatever you do don't
sleep on yourself, stay woke

TO HAIKU'M IT MAY CONCERN
Living Your Best Life Even When Mercury is in Retrograde

Sometimes it looks

like it's falling apart

when it's falling into place

Harvey Fitz

It takes a lot but
when you serve the supplier
the burden is light

Harvey Fitz

I've only ever

been scared of one person my

entire life... me

Harvey Fitz

Your petty has a
shelf life. When it gets old you
turn miserable

Harvey Fitz

It's incredible
to finally meet who you
were meant to become

Harvey Fitz

Insecurity
mixed with intimidation
will breed a hater

People will drive
you crazy only if
you hand them over the keys.

Harvey Fitz

Maybe God removed

them cause He knows how toxic

they are to your growth

CHAPTER 2 LAUGH

How are you riding
on E while smoking a blunt?
you bought the wrong gas!

What do you call an
ex from the state
Maryland? an old bae get it?

Harvey Fitz

TO HAIKU'M IT MAY CONCERN
Living Your Best Life Even When Mercury is in Retrograde

He actually
likes cuddling but your lace-
front smells like pure death sis

Harvey Fitz

She actually
likes giving head but you don't
wipe your ass well bruh

Consistency will

get your dick sucked like it was

dipped in oxtail juice

TO HAIKU'M IT MAY CONCERN
Living Your Best Life Even When Mercury is in Retrograde

Y'all stood those brooms up
and the world went straight to hell
in a handbasket

Harvey Fitz

Drink lots of water
eat all your vegetables
mind your own business

TO HAIKU'M IT MAY CONCERN
Living Your Best Life Even When Mercury is in Retrograde

I have accepted
the fact that I am the
"Why are you like this?!" friend

Harvey Fitz

Fitteds are to men
what lacefronts are to women
they will transform us

Harvey Fitz

I just want someone

to look at me the way

Drake did Jake from State Farm

Never argue with
someone who leaves the "s" off
the word specific

If the Bible were
written today WAP would be
Song of Solomon

A lot of them are
living their best lives because
someone pays their bills

Don't forget to roll
your R's on Enrique Mas
it's a GOLDEN rule

Sticking your hand out
the door is not a good
way to check the weather

So what y'all season
your tubs with? I use a
lil Ajax and Comet

If your queer ass loves
Chick Fil 'A isn't that
like negative feedback?

TO HAIKU'M IT MAY CONCERN
Living Your Best Life Even When Mercury is in Retrograde

My music playlist
is extremely diverse
from Meg Mac to Meek Mill

Harvey Fitz

Wash your meat before
you cook it and wash your legs
while in the shower

CHAPTER 3 LOVE

Make sure you are not

changing yourself for

people who don't know themselves

If they don't challenge
you to be your best self
then you're with the wrong one

Plot twist if you don't
ever become better
then you are the wrong one

Be the one who
brings clarity to your
spouse's life not confusion

Sometimes the thought that

counts is counting against

you make sure it adds up

Social media
single is not the same
thing as real life single

If it costs you your
peace of mind then it's not
worth the price or your time

Do-overs for those
who treat you like leftovers
will give you heartburn

61
Harvey Fitz

It's not the baggage
so much as how the
baggage is being handled

Harvey Fitz

Cuffing season is

also fuckboy season

so please buyer beware

Whole time I've been an

entire meal out here but

now I believe it

Harvey Fitz

You don't really miss
me you're just horny and saw
my green light was on

Harvey Fitz

A brown sugary

Wakandan Luv Jones is what

I deserve from you

Harvey Fitz

TO HAIKU'M IT MAY CONCERN
Living Your Best Life Even When Mercury is in Retrograde

You drew first blood from
my heart and painted
pretty little lies with it

Harvey Fitz

You must be tired
dating him and raising him
are both full time jobs

If you are black and
also a Trump supporter you don't
love yourself

When I hear him
speak it reminds me
why I fell in love with his mind

Harvey Fitz

Shift your focus from
boyfriend/girlfriend and rent to
marriage and mortgage

Harvey Fitz

Please stop giving the

best parts of you to the worst

possible people

Harvey Fitz

Your heart deserves more
than just some half assed part time
lover please know that

Harvey Fitz

One minute you hate

his guts the next minute

he's in your guts how Sway?

TO HAIKU'M IT MAY CONCERN
Living Your Best Life Even When Mercury is in Retrograde

Always know where you
stand in case the rug gets pulled
out from under you

Harvey Fitz

You ain't no angel
and I ain't no saint but our
love should be sacred

Harvey Fitz

TO HAIKU'M IT MAY CONCERN
Living Your Best Life Even When Mercury is in Retrograde

I'm a good person
and I deserve the love that
my heart has to give

77
Harvey Fitz

Loving you was like
biting your tongue while eating
something really good

The thing with second
chances is you never get
the same heart again

Love me or leave me
the hell alone said
every last Aquarius

Harvey Fitz

You treated my heart
like loose change and told me to
charge it to the game

Harvey Fitz

They were at peace when
you met them so don't come in
here disturbing it

The bullets that we
dodge are sometimes beautiful
and really mean well

Harvey Fitz

You will love again
right now just focus on the
process of healing

Harvey Fitz

CHAPTER 4 REPEAT

Actions speak louder

than words and patterns are the

voice of reasoning

TO HAIKU'M IT MAY CONCERN
Living Your Best Life Even When Mercury is in Retrograde

The spirits will not
leave your home because you sage
with the windows closed

Harvey Fitz

Toxic is toxic
is toxic regardless
how less toxic it seems

Harvey Fitz

Blood is thicker than
water but even blood
may need to be transfused

TO HAIKU'M IT MAY CONCERN
Living Your Best Life Even When Mercury is in Retrograde

We built this nation
and carry it on our backs
get off of our necks

Harvey Fitz

Stop giving your fears
so much credit and
defer those payments to hope

Harvey Fitz

Stop arguing with
people who need wifi
in order to reply

Harvey Fitz

Bright ideas and
big dreams without plans or
goals are moot talking points

Do not go to the
circus if you're tired of
getting played by clowns

Harvey Fitz

Sometimes the heart takes
the long way home in which case
the love grows fonder

Harvey Fitz

I forgive you but
my price has gone up since you
last wasted my time

Harvey Fitz

Don't let your child go
fatherless because you
want to prove a point sis

When the blessing is
contingent on your leap
of faith you better jump

Harvey Fitz

TO HAIKU'M IT MAY CONCERN
Living Your Best Life Even When Mercury is in Retrograde

You better sharpen
your eyes because the wolves
are tailoring their fleece

Harvey Fitz

Stop doubting yourself
you're already dope
enough the journey awaits

Harvey Fitz

TO HAIKU'M IT MAY CONCERN
Living Your Best Life Even When Mercury is in Retrograde

I wish my student
loan debt was forgiven as
fast as Amber was

101
Harvey Fitz

I may not be your
cup of tea but someone
else will get their thirst quenched

Harvey Fitz

Time heals all wounds
but if the wound
improperly heals then time's wasted

Harvey Fitz

Persistence in the
face of doubt produces
the strength you need to thrive

Harvey Fitz

Be the person that
everybody wants to
fuck instead of has fucked

If you don't want it
more than you doubt yourself then
you'll never have it

Harvey Fitz

I am the friend who
"Hey I got you on speaker"
doesn't mean shit to

Harvey Fitz

While you're scared to take
that leap of faith Burger
King is making tacos

Harvey Fitz

TO HAIKU'M IT MAY CONCERN
Living Your Best Life Even When Mercury is in Retrograde

Strive daily to make
it back home with all the
fucks you left the house with

Harvey Fitz

Sometimes you have to
change in order to
receive what you're waiting on

Harvey Fitz

No voodoo performed

through this Popeye's sandwich shall

prosper against me

Harvey Fitz

It is not your job
to make sense of the
favor on your life to them

Harvey Fitz

Let them sleep on you
soon they'll be dreaming of the
chance to work with you

Harvey Fitz

You might want to cut
off those people who need you
more than they love you

Harvey Fitz

The weapons may

form may even sting

a little but they won't prosper

Someone's breakthrough is
tied to your triumph so
please do not give up now

Don't be so anxious
remember you are
birthing elephant sized feats

Alabama why
weren't you this pro-life when
Black folks were getting lynched?

Harvey Fitz

Direction is more
important than speed so stop
going nowhere fast

It can be tempting to

sacrifice quality for quantity. Don't

Apologies for
hate speech stemming from the
heart are huge wastes of breath

Harvey Fitz

Sometimes a quick fix

will worsen the

damages steady your paces

Harvey Fitz

May God provide a
ram every time a jackass
tries to hinder you

Harvey Fitz

Don't ever let the
sunburned stop you from shining
your light is too bright

Harvey Fitz

TO HAIKU'M IT MAY CONCERN
Living Your Best Life Even When Mercury is in Retrograde

What are your
motives for poetry
are they pure or for clout and fame?

Harvey Fitz

My soul is not for
sale and my peace of mind is
not to be disturbed

Harvey Fitz

Some of you will die

in your potential

because of your fear of change

Harvey Fitz

We owe it to our

selves as well as those

watching to keep on going

Harvey Fitz

ABOUT THE AUTHOR

Sir Harvey Fitz is an Alexandria, Virginia native and a graduate of Virginia State University with a BA in Mass Communications: Radio & Television Production. He currently resides in the Washington Metropolitan Area and is a freelance photographer, theatrically trained actor, and spoken word artist. Harvey has photographed a number of concerts, events, and notable figures and is passionate about documenting people in everyday life. He has written and performed spoken word poetry for over 10 years and has been acting ever since early childhood. He was also a part of a small group of students and professors at Virginia State University that revived its theatre organization and program and as a result his Alma mater has been ranked among the top HBCU's for studies in the arts. In his leisure time Harvey can be found in a local library lost in a book, or at a festival or farmer's market with his Canon DSLR shooting guerilla style.

send all inquiries to info@harveyfitz.com

Made in the USA
Middletown, DE
02 October 2023

39960717R00077